Five
Loaves
for Levi

Written *by* Bob Hartman
Illustrated by Michael McGuire

For Ben, who'd rather have hot cakes and sausage. B.H.

To Phillip for being the real *Levi.* M.M.

VICTOR BOOKS
A Division of Scripture Press Publications Inc.

What was it like in the belly of Ben's brother?
It was gurgling.
A whole day had passed since breakfast.
And in that time Levi and his big brother
Ben had climbed to the top of the hill,
wrestled around in the grass, chased after
a careless snake, and then joined the crowd
to listen to Jesus, The Teacher.
But now little Levi's stomach was talking to him,
gurgling ever so gently, reminding him
of how hungry he was.
Levi tugged at the robe of his big brother Ben,
but Ben just shrugged it off.
What was it like in the belly of Ben's brother?
It was gurgling.

What was it like in the belly of Ben's brother?

It was grumbling.

"Your Father in heaven takes care of the birds," said the Teacher. "He takes care of the flowers. Don't you think He can take care of you?"

Then he stopped to take a breath, and everything went quiet: the adults, the children, even the birds—waiting for his next word.

Everything, that is, but the belly of Ben's brother.

"Grumble," went Levi's belly.

"Mumble," it continued.

"Rumble," it went on.

Till somebody giggled, and someone else snickered, and Ben had to turn around, embarrassed, and tell his brother off.

"Quiet!" he whispered.

"But I'm hungry," sulked Levi.

What was it like in the belly of Ben's brother?

It was grumbling.

What was it like in the belly of Ben's brother?

It was growling.

Levi could hardly pay attention.

His stomach was complaining every minute now.

Feed me. Feed Me! FEED ME!!

His big brother had some food. Levi had watched

their mother pack it up that very morning.

Five fresh loaves of bread. And two dried fish.

Levi looked at the lunch bag. Then he looked at Ben.

Ben was watching the Teacher. This was Levi's chance!

Gingerly, he reached for the lunch bag.

And then "Growl!" went his belly, louder than ever.

Ben grabbed the bag, scowled at his brother,
and only half-whispered this time,
"Mother put me in charge of the food,
and I say we wait until the story is over!"
Then he wrapped his arms around the bag
and turned back to listen.
Levi's stomach growled one more time.
"Oh, be quiet," he growled back.
What was it like in the
belly of Ben's brother?
It was groaning.
Levi grabbed his tummy
He rocked back and forth. And just
when he thought he could take no more . . .
the Teacher finished.
All around him, people stood and stretched
and talked about how wonderful
Jesus' words had been. But Levi could
think of only one thing: FOOD.

"Time to eat!" he announced. "Now give me the bag, Ben."
Levi started to unlock Ben's fingers, when his brother nodded,
     "All right, all right. I'm hungry too."
     Ben let go of the bag and began to unpack it.
"One loaf for me." he counted. "One loaf for you."

Levi's stomach groaned again, and Levi groaned
with it. His brother was always dividing
things up. One for me. One for you.
But somehow Ben's "one" always turned
out bigger. Well, not this time, Levi decided.
But just as he grabbed hold of the lunch bag,
and opened it, someone interrupted.

"Excuse me, boys," said the man.
"My name is Andrew and I'm one of
the Teacher's helpers. We have
a lot of hungry people here—
five thousand, at least.
But it seems that no one brought
anything to eat. Well, no one
but you two."

Levi's stomach groaned again.
"Please, no," he thought.
"Don't let him ask what I think
he's going to ask. A piece for Ben,
a piece for me, and a piece for
everybody else?
I won't even get a crumb!"

But just as Levi opened his mouth, his brother
     spoke, "There you go," Ben said. He took
     the bag from Levi and handed over
     their lunch. "Take it. If Jesus
     wants it, He can have it."
Andrew thanked them and walked
     quickly away, while Levi
     watched his dinner disappear.
"I know what you're gonna say,"
     Ben warned, "but mother put
     me in charge of the lunch."
So Levi said nothing. He just
     groaned along with his
     empty tummy.

What was it like in the belly of Ben's brother?

It was glum.

His lunch was lost, and with five thousand mouths to feed,
he'd never get it back. Levi didn't know whether
to run off after Andrew, smack his big brother
in the eye, or just sit there and cry.

Ben tried to be helpful.

"Look, Levi," he explained, "I know you're hungry, but,
remember what Jesus said about the birds and the
flowers and how God can take care of us, too."

It didn't help. Levi just glared at him.

And that's when Andrew returned.

"Here you go, boys. I thought you ought to get the first portions."

And he set down before them a pile of bread and fish.

"You mean you're giving us our lunch back?"

Levi stuttered. "You didn't need it?"

"Well . . ." Andrew smiled awkwardly," Yes we did need it.
Somehow, and don't ask me how, Jesus took your
lunch and prayed over it and then started
breaking it into pieces. And before
you know it, we had enough bread
and fish to feed everybody here.
Pretty amazing, isn't it?"

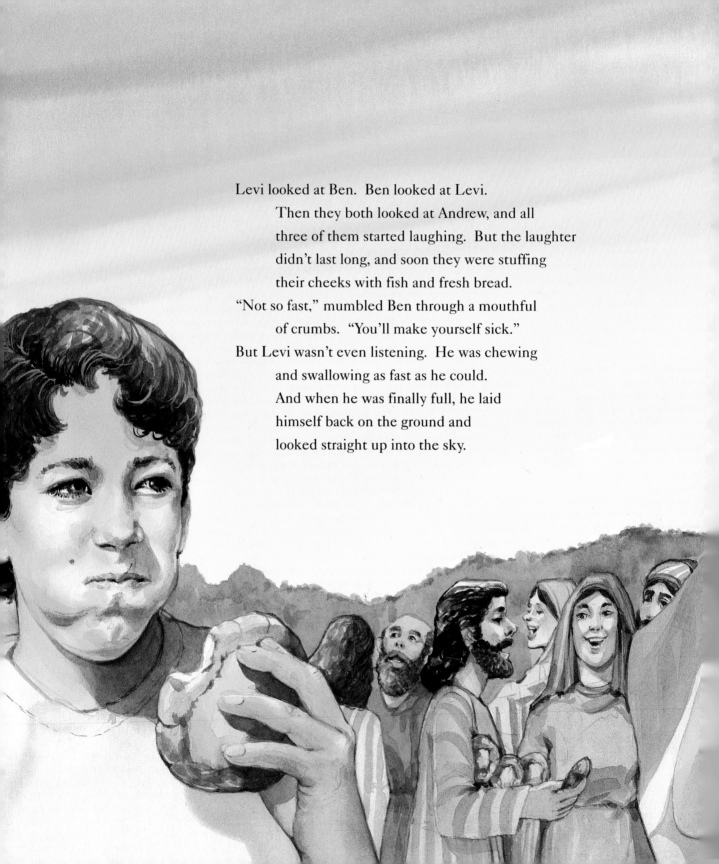

Levi looked at Ben. Ben looked at Levi.
Then they both looked at Andrew, and all
three of them started laughing. But the laughter
didn't last long, and soon they were stuffing
their cheeks with fish and fresh bread.
"Not so fast," mumbled Ben through a mouthful
of crumbs. "You'll make yourself sick."
But Levi wasn't even listening. He was chewing
and swallowing as fast as he could.
And when he was finally full, he laid
himself back on the ground and
looked straight up into the sky.

He was gorged. He was glutted!
Then a bird flew by, and he remembered
Jesus' words. The Teacher was right, after all—
the One who took care of the birds and flowers
had taken care of him as well.
Then Levi patted his bursting belly and shut his eyes.
"Thank-you, Father in Heaven." he whispered.
What was it like in the belly of Ben's brother?
It was grateful. It was glad!

The story you have just read is based on the Luke 6:30-44.

Art direction: Paul Higdon/Grace K. Chan Mallette
Production: Myrna Hasse
Editing: Liz Morton Duckworth

1 2 3 4 5 6 7 8 9 10 Printing/Year 98 97 96 95 94

VICTOR BOOKS
A division of SP Publications, Inc.
Wheaton, Illinois 60187